Extraordinary
ANIMALS

Published in 2013 by Wayland
Copyright © Wayland 2013

Wayland
338 Euston Road
London NW1 3BH

Wayland Australia
Level 17/207 Kent Street
Sydney, NSW 2000

Produced for Wayland by Calcium: www.calciumcreative.co.uk
Design: Simon Borrough
Editor: Sarah Eason
Picture researcher: Susannah Jayes
Commissioning Editor for Wayland: Victoria Brooker

Picture Acknowledgments: Ardea: John Cancalosi 23, Pat Morris 6; Corbis:
Frans Lanting 30, 32, 38; Brian Gratwicke 17; Photolibrary: N Howell 31,
Neeraj Misthra 39, Robert Tyrrell 26; Rex Features: Greenpeace 8; Shutterstock:
bierchen 12, James Blinn 5tr, 10, BMCL 20, BlueOrangeStudio 33, Cigdem Sean
Cooper 9, Ant Clausen 29, H.Damke 28, dezignor 14, Mark Doherty 11, Peter
Graham 34, Joel Bauchat Grant 42, Kjersti Joergensen 5br, 7, 37, Gail Johnson 43,
J Klingebiel 41, Hugh Landsdown 13, Domen Lombergar 15, Luis Louro 4tr, 16,
Steve Lovegrove 4br, 18, Lukich 36, Bruce MacQueen 25, Marcin Miemiec 4bl,
22, Christian Musat 35, Dmitry V Petrenko 21, think4photop 27, Turtleman 19,
worldswildlifewonders 3, 24, 40.

British Library Cataloguing in Publication Data
        Gray, Leon, 1974-
        Extraordinary animals.
        1. Animals--Juvenile literature.
        I. Title
        590-dc22

ISBN: 978 0 7502 7161 5

Printed in China
Wayland is a division of Hachette Children's Books,
an Hachette UK company.

www.hachette.co.uk

Contents

Amazing animals

The world is full of weird and wonderful animals of all different shapes and sizes. Some are huge but harmless and others are tiny but deadly. In this book, you will meet some of the world's most extraordinary animals, from fish with sharp spikes and venomous spines, to monkeys with huge noses and brightly coloured bottoms.

Poison dart frog

Some animals may look fairly normal but feed in strange ways, such as the rodents that eat their own poo, and the ravenous Komodo dragon which can gobble up to 80 per cent of its body weight in one meal.

Then there are the animals that are strange beyond belief, such as the salamanders that can grow new body parts, the duck-billed platypus – an egg-laying mammal with a bird-like beak – and the fish that looks like a grumpy uncle!

Hornbill

Thorny devil

4

Animal groups

Scientists like to organize similar animals into groups, so this book is ordered in a similar way. There are five main groups of animals that have a backbone (scientists call them **vertebrates**). They are: fish; **amphibians** such as frogs and salamanders; **reptiles** such as lizards and snakes; birds; and **mammals**.

Leafy sea dragon

Fish are **cold-blooded** creatures that live in water and breathe using **gills**.

Amphibians are cold-blooded animals that live in the water when they are young and then dramatically change into adults that live on land.

Reptiles are scaly creatures with cold blood.

Birds are **warm-blooded** animals with feathers and wings that help them to fly.

Mammals are warm-blooded animals, usually with fur, that feed their young with milk.

Proboscis monkey

Hagfish

Hagfish are a group of fish-like animals. They have long, eel-like bodies and paddle-shaped tails. What makes these creatures unusual is the way they ooze slime to escape from their enemies. The slime makes their bodies very slippery. Hagfish can also tie their bodies into knots. **Predators** find it really hard to hold on to them.

Location deep oceans around the world

Adult size 50cm long

Diet carnivore

Feeding time

Hagfish feed on dead and dying animals in the sea. They grab on to their food using tiny 'teeth' that line their mouth. They rip off chunks of flesh by twisting and turning their bodies as they feed.

A slimy hagfish rests on the seabed. These ugly sea creatures keep the ocean clean by eating dead animals.

FREAKY FEATURE

Hagfish are so long and thin that they can slip inside the bodies of their **prey** and eat them from the inside out!

Scorpion fish

Scorpion fish are a group of fish that use **venom** to protect themselves from predators. They lie on the ocean floor, waiting for passing prey such as small fish. Some, such as the stonefish, are masters of disguise – they can change colour to blend in with their surroundings. Others, such as the lionfish, are brightly coloured to warn other sea creatures to keep away!

Venomous spines

The stonefish is the world's most venomous fish. Deadly spines on its back are coated with venom. The spines stick up when the stonefish feels threatened. The fish is well **camouflaged** on the seabed, so divers can easily step on their spines without realizing it.

The bright red colour of this scorpion fish warns other sea creatures that it is dangerous.

Location shallow coastal waters in **tropical** regions; some live in rivers

Number of species 350

Diet carnivore

A DEADLY INJECTION

The scorpion fish's venom is so powerful, it can kill a person!

Blobfish

The blobfish is one of the ugliest fish alive! It lives so deep in the ocean that people rarely get to see it. We only know it exists because deep-sea fishermen bring it to the surface in their nets.

Location deep waters around Australia

Adult size up to 30cm long

Diet omnivore

Blobbing along

Unlike most fish, the blobfish does not have a sac of air inside its body to help it float. Instead, its jelly-like body is slightly less heavy than water, so it floats just above the seabed. Instead of swimming after prey, the blobfish drifts in the ocean **currents** and eats anything that passes by.

The miserable-looking blobfish is on the brink of extinction because so many are becoming trapped in fishing nets. Photos of the blobfish are almost as rare as the fish itself.

8

Puffer fish

Puffer fish protect themselves from predators in a very special way. They are slow swimmers, so they cannot get away from predators such as sharks. Instead, they puff up their body into a ball! They do this by swallowing air or water and storing it in their stomach. When they have ballooned, sharp spines also appear on their back. If any predator takes a mouthful, they choke!

Location mainly tropical waters around the world

Number of species 120

Diet omnivore

The starry puffer fish is covered with black spots. As the fish grows, more black spots appear on its skin.

Poison protection

Some puffer fish have a dangerous poison in their bodies. If predators do try to take a bite, they're in trouble. This deadly poison can kill people. One puffer fish has enough poison in its body to kill up to 30 people.

A DANGEROUS MEAL

In Japan, some puffer fish are a luxury food. Only experienced chefs can prepare the fish, so that the diners aren't fatally poisoned!

Leafy sea dragon

The leafy sea dragon hardly looks like a fish at all. Leaf-like flaps of skin stick out of its body, making it look like a piece of floating seaweed. This makes it hard to spot in the water. It can also change colour to blend in with its surroundings. Leafy sea dragons drift in the ocean currents, and move around by beating the tiny fins on their back and neck.

Meet the parents

The female leafy sea dragon lays up to 250 eggs, but it is the male who then looks after them, on a special pouch on his tail. The eggs are pink at first, but turn purple or orange when the young are ready to **hatch**. The male rubs his tail on rocks and plants to help free the babies from his pouch.

Location west coast of Australia

Adult size about 22cm long

Diet carnivore

These leafy sea dragons are masters of disguise. They look like pieces of seaweed floating in the ocean currents.

Hammerhead shark

Hammerhead sharks take their name from their strangely shaped heads, which are flattened into a hammer shape. This helps them to sense prey, because their eyes are on each side of their head so they can see in all directions. They also have special sense **organs** in their head to help them track down their prey as it moves.

Stingray supper

Stingrays are a favourite food of hammerhead sharks. Stingrays hide under the sandy seabed, but the hammerhead uses its senses to follow the stingray's movements under the sand. The hammerhead then moves in for the kill, using its wide head to pin down the fish on the seabed.

SHARK FIN SOUP

In some countries, people eat shark fin soup, which is usually made from the fins of the hammerhead shark.

Location warm waters around the world

Adult size up to 9m long

Diet carnivore

The odd-shaped head of the hammerhead shark is an **adaptation** to help it find its favourite prey – stingrays.

Angler fish

Some angler fish have a fleshy lobe of skin, to attract prey. This weird feature hangs from a spine on the fish's head, a bit like **bait** on a fishing rod. The angler fish shakes the spine, making the lobe wriggle like a worm. As prey animals come close to the angler fish's mouth, it snaps shut on them!

Location oceans around the world

Number of species more than 200

Diet carnivore

The fins of this yellow angler fish have tiny 'fingers' which the fish uses to creep along the seabed.

Bizarre breeding

Some deep-sea angler fish breed in an unusual way. Several males grip on to the female's body using their sharp teeth. Gradually, the males become part of the female's body – losing their eyes and major body parts! All that are left are their reproductive parts, which are used to make the next generation of angler fish.

Mudskipper

The mudskipper is equally at home on the land as in the water. It uses its fins like legs to walk on the sandy shore.

FREAKY FEATURE

Male mudskippers show off to females by doing push-ups on their front fins. They also leap in the air and flip over to attract a mate.

Location shallow water and coastal areas

Adult size 10–30cm long

Diet carnivore

Mudskippers are unusual fish because they can survive on land as well as in water. They have gills to breathe in water, but on land they breathe through their skin. This only works if their skin is wet, so the mudskipper needs to stay near water to survive. It also stores water behind its ears to prevent its gills from drying out.

Walking fish

The mudskipper is named for the way it 'skips' across the mud, using its front fins as legs. Even when these fish are under the water, they spend a lot of time crawling on the sea floor in search of prey such as worms and **crustaceans**.

13

Axolotl

All amphibians start life as a **larva** that hatches from an egg. The larva lives in water and breathes using gills. In most amphibians, the larva develops into an adult that lives on the land and breathes using lungs. But this does not happen to the axolotl. It keeps all the features of the larva, such as gills, but it can produce young of its own.

FREAKY FEATURE

Axolotls are unusual because they can grow new body parts.

The feathery gills on the side of the axolotl's body help it to breathe under the water.

Location central Mexico

Adult size around 20cm long

Diet carnivore

Saving the species

Axolotls come from two lakes in central Mexico. These lakes are now very dirty and much smaller than they once were, so there are few axolotls left in the wild. But many people keep axolotls as pets. Scientists also keep them for **research**.

Olm

Olms live in dark caves, so they do not need good eyesight. In fact, they are almost blind. Olms rely on their senses of smell and hearing to find their way around and track down their prey, such as crabs and snails. The olm's skin is so pale you can see its insides through it!

Water dwellers

Olms spend all of their lives in water. They have long, slender bodies, thin fins and short legs. Unlike most amphibians, olms do not leave the water to breed but keep their gills to breathe. The gills appear bright red because the blood shows through the olm's pale skin.

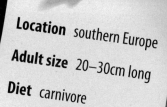

Location southern Europe

Adult size 20–30cm long

Diet carnivore

The olm spends all of its life in underground rivers. The bright pink gills near the olm's head help it to breathe under the water.

FAMOUS FISH

The famous British scientist Charles Darwin studied the olm and wrote about it in his book 'On the Origin of Species'. He thought the olm was a good example of how animals **evolve**, or change over time.

Poison dart frog

Poison dart frogs come in many different colours – from blue and green to gold and black. Their colours warn other animals that they are poisonous, so beware! Their poison is used by local people on the darts they shoot at their prey, to kill it.

Parental care

Some male poison dart frogs make good parents. They carry their eggs and **tadpoles** on their backs, fixing them in place with a sticky gel. The frog then crawls through the rainforest and puts the tadpoles in the pools of water that collect in the leaves of plants. The tadpoles feed on small insects and develop into adult frogs.

Location Central and South America

Adult size most species are around 1.5cm long

Diet carnivore

The bright colours of the dyeing dart frog warn other animals that it is poisonous and should not be eaten.

16

FREAKY FEATURE

One tiny golden poison dart frog has enough venom in its body to kill ten people.

Giant salamander

Giant salamanders are the largest amphibians in the world. There are three species: the hellbender, the Chinese giant salamander and the Japanese giant salamander. The hellbender lives in ponds and streams in the United States. The Chinese and Japanese giant salamanders live in similar **habitats** in southern Asia.

Location ponds and streams in the United States, China and Japan

Adult size around 1.5m long

Diet carnivore

Life underwater

Giant salamanders spend most of their time in the water, where they eat insects, fish, frogs and crabs. Under the water, giant salamanders breathe through their skin, which has many folds to help them take in more air. On land, they breathe through lungs.

The Chinese giant salamander can live for more than 75 years in **captivity**.

17

Thorny devil

The thorny devil is a lizard named because of the spikes that cover its back and neck, and the two thorny scales on its head, which look like the horns of a devil. The sharp spikes help to keep predators away.

Location Australia

Adult size up to 20cm long

Diet carnivore

The brown colours of the thorny devil provide it with camouflage.

Where is the water?

The thorny devil lives in the Australian **outback**, where there is little water. It collects water from the cool night air as dew on its body. The water runs down the grooves between its spines and into its mouth.

FREAKY FEATURE

The thorny devil's main food is ants. One lizard can eat up to a thousand ants in a day!

Gharial

The gharial is a large relative of alligators and crocodiles. It has long, narrow jaws, lined with lots of razor-sharp teeth. The male gharial has a rounded growth, called a *ghara* (the Hindi word for 'pot'), at the tip of its snout.

At risk

Gharials were once common in the rivers of southern Asia, but today they are almost **extinct**. Back in the 1970s, things were so bad that scientists counted fewer than 60 gharials in the wild. They are now protected by laws in many countries, and more are surviving in the wild again.

This reptile uses its sharp teeth to grab hold of slippery fish.

Location rivers in India and Nepal

Adult size about 5m long

Diet carnivore

19

Frill-necked lizard

The most amazing thing about the frill-necked lizard is the large flap of skin around its neck, which it stretches out to frighten predators. The lizard gapes its mouth wide open when it feels threatened. Thin spines connect its jaws to its neck frill, so this makes the frill flare out when the lizard opens wide.

Body temperature

Like other reptiles, the frill-necked lizard is a cold-blooded creature. It needs to lie out in the sun to warm up, so it can stay active. In the morning or early afternoon, the frill-necked lizard climbs down from the treetops and sunbathes out in the open. Scientists also think that the lizard uses its neck frill to help it warm up or cool down.

Location Australia and New Guinea

Adult size up to 90cm long

Diet carnivore

FRILLED MASCOT

A frill-necked lizard named Lizzie was the mascot for the 2000 Paralympic Games in Sydney, Australia.

This frill-necked lizard fans out the flap of skin around its neck as a warning to predators.

Komodo dragon

Location South-east Asia

Adult size 2.5m long

Diet carnivore

The Komodo dragon is the main predator on a string of small islands that form part of Indonesia in South-east Asia. (Komodo is the name of one of these islands.) These huge lizards hunt birds and small mammals. The Komodo hides and waits for the right moment, then bursts out and chases down its prey with a short burst of speed.

The Komodo dragon is the largest lizard in the world. This Komodo is sunbathing to warm its massive body.

Deadly bite

The Komodo does not always kill its victim when it attacks. When it bites, its sharp teeth rip through its prey. Saliva from the Komodo's mouth contains **bacteria** that infect the wounds. Even if the prey escapes, it usually dies from the **infection** a few days later. The Komodo then uses its sense of smell to sniff out the dead or dying animal.

FREAKY FEATURE

A Komodo dragon can eat almost 80 per cent of its own body weight in one meal.

21

Hornbill

Hornbills come in many different shapes and sizes, but they all have an unusual, downward-curving bill. They use these for many jobs, such as building nests, **preening** their feathers, fighting and catching prey such as insects. The bill is so large and heavy that the hornbill has special bones and strong muscles in its neck to support it.

Calling card

Most hornbills have a bony growth, called a casque, on their bills. In some species the casque is very small, but in others it is large and hollow. Hornbills use their casque to make their calls louder.

Location Africa and Asia

Number of species more than 55

Diet omnivore

The wrinkled hornbill lives in the rainforests of South-east Asia. These birds never drink – they get all the water they need from food.

FREAKY FEATURE

Some hornbills have solid casques, which they use as battering rams in fights with other hornbills.

Mallee fowl

Location south-western Australia

Adult size about 60cm long

Diet omnivore

The mallee fowl is a stocky **game bird** that lives in the dry **scrubland** of south-western Australia. They are shy birds, and spend most of their day looking for food on the ground. If they sense danger, they stop dead in their tracks. They are well camouflaged, so predators find them hard to spot. If a mallee fowl is attacked, it flies up into to the nearest tree.

Egg incubator

The most unusual thing about the mallee fowl is the way it lays its eggs in a huge pile of mud and rotting vegetation. The males spend several months building this mound, which can reach an impressive size – up to 50 metres across and 1 metre deep. The female then lays her eggs in a hollow in the centre of it. The heat given off by the rotting plants keeps the eggs cosy and warm, until the young hatch from them.

The Australian mallee fowl builds one of the largest nests of any bird.

Harpy eagle

The harpy eagle is a huge, powerful **bird of prey** – in fact, it is the biggest bird of prey in the Americas. The females usually weigh twice as much as the males! The harpy eagle's wingspan is much smaller than on other birds the same size. This makes it possible for it to dart expertly through the trees in its forest habitat.

Location Central and South America

Adult size up to 1m long with a wingspan of up to 1.8m

Diet carnivore

Killing machine

The harpy eagle is a fearsome predator. It has a sharp, hooked beak, and feet armed with talons up to 20 centimetres long! It is so big and powerful that it can pluck mammals as big as monkeys and sloths from the treetops.

NATIONAL BIRD

The harpy eagle is the **national bird of Panama**. It is shown on the country's coat of arms.

The sharp, hooked beak of this Costa Rican harpy eagle is perfectly suited for ripping flesh from its prey.

Wild turkey

The wild turkey is the same species as the captive turkeys we eat, but unlike captive turkeys, wild turkeys can fly. Centuries ago, the Aztec people of Mexico kept wild turkeys for their meat and eggs. Native Americans also used wild turkey feathers to decorate their **headdresses**.

Location United States and Mexico

Adult size males 1m or more; females around 80cm long

Diet omnivore

Ugly birds

Turkeys are known for being ugly, because of the fleshy flaps of skin on the head and neck of the male birds. When the males become excited, these fill with blood and almost cover their whole head. The males use this feature to show off to females during the **breeding season**.

A male wild turkey struts his stuff, fanning his tail to impress a mate.

Bee hummingbird

There are many different hummingbirds, and they are all tiny, but the bee hummingbird is the smallest of all. The females are just six centimetres long, and weigh less than a few grains of rice! The males are even smaller! No wonder the females lay tiny eggs, too. They are each about the size of a pea!

This bee hummingbird is perching on the end of a pencil, which shows exactly how tiny it is.

Super flyer

Hummingbirds are masters of flight – they can fly backwards, and even upside-down by rapidly beating their wings in a figure-of-eight pattern. Hummingbirds can also hover in the air, using their long, pointed bill to suck up sugary **nectar** from flowers. These birds catch tiny insects as they dart among the trees.

Location Cuba

Adult size 5cm

Diet omnivore

FREAKY FEATURE

The tiny bee hummingbird beats its wings faster than any other bird – up to 80 times every second.

Peafowl

Location India and Pakistan

Adult size around 2m long

Diet omnivore

Peafowl live in forests and spend most of the day on the ground, where they look for food such as fruit, insects and small vertebrates (animals with a backbone). They fly up to the treetops to **roost** and to escape from predators.

Tail display

Peafowl are known for the amazing feather display of the males, or peacocks. The peacock fans out his long train of feathers to attract females, or peahens. The feathers stretch out from the peacock's back, shining in the light. Each feather ends with a brightly coloured eyespot. Although the tail feathers attract females, they also attract predators. Luckily the male is strong enough to fight off most predators that might attack it.

The peafowl is the national bird of India.

Capybara

The capybara is the world's largest rodent – the same type of animal as rats and mice. Capybaras spend a lot of time in the water, and their bodies are perfectly suited to it. For example, their eyes, ears and nostrils are on the top of their head. This means they can see, hear and breathe while almost completely underwater.

Clever fur

The heavy, barrel-shaped body of the capybara is also covered with a layer of thick fur. Its outer layer is waterproof and keeps the capybara dry. The fine under layer keeps the capybara warm in cooler water.

Location South America

Adult size 1.3m long

Diet herbivore

FREAKY FEATURE

Capybara's feet are slightly webbed – like a duck's. This helps them to swim

The thick fur of the water-loving capybara keeps the animal warm and dry. It also protects the capybara from sunburn.

Dugong

The dugong is an unusual sea mammal that lives in warm, tropical seas. Like other sea mammals, such as dolphins and whales, a dugong's body is adapted for swimming. The paddle-like front limbs and fluked tail (shaped like a dolphin's) help to propel the dugong through the water.

Grazing grasses

Dugongs are often called 'sea cows' because they eat mainly one thing – plants called sea grasses. Sea grasses cover the seabed in the coastal waters where the dugong lives.

DUGONGS IN ART

A dugong is shown in a cave painting that was made more than 5000 years ago. The ancient artwork was found in Tambun Cave in Ipoh, Malaysia, in 1959.

Location oceans off East Africa and southern Asia

Adult size 2.7m long

Diet herbivore

Dugongs paddle along the seabed searching for sea grass to eat.

29

Naked mole rat

Location East Africa

Adult size up to 10cm long

Diet herbivore

Naked mole rats live in underground **burrows** beneath the deserts of eastern Africa. They are well suited to underground life. They have no hair, and huge front teeth which they use to dig tunnels. Their tube-shaped body and short legs help them to move along the tunnels easily.

The naked mole rat uses its huge front teeth to dig burrows beneath the hot African deserts.

FREAKY FEATURE

The naked mole rat has poor eyesight. Instead, it uses its long whiskers to feel its way around in the darkness.

Life in the colony

These ugly animals are one of only a few mammals that live in groups called **colonies**. Each colony has about 80 naked mole rats. Only one female breeds with two or three males. All the other naked mole rats act as workers, helping the mother to raise her babies and finding food for the colony.

Star-nosed mole

The star-nosed mole is a weird-looking mammal. Its 'star nose' is a fleshy growth made up of 11 pairs of tentacles. The star-nosed mole lives under the ground and has poor eyesight, so its nose growth is its main sense organ. Sensitive to touch, it helps the mole to feel its way around in the dark and find food, such as earthworms and insects.

Digging underground

Star-nosed moles burrow underground, and use their huge, spade-like front legs and amazingly long claws for digging tunnels.

The star-nosed mole is a digging machine, with huge spade-like front feet and a touch-sensitive nose.

Location Canada and the United States

Adult size up to 20cm long

Diet carnivore

Aye-aye

The aye-aye is a type of lemur –
a relative of **primates** such as
monkeys, apes and even people.
The odd-looking aye-aye spends
almost all of its life in the treetops
of the rainforest in Madagascar.
During the day, it curls up in a
nest of leaves and branches. At
night it comes out to find food.

Location Madagascar

Adult size up to 1m long
from head to tail

Diet omnivore

Hooking a meal

The aye-aye has an amazing way
of finding its food. It uses its long
middle finger to tap on tree trunks,
then it listens carefully for insect grubs
moving beneath the bark. If it hears
something, the aye-aye uses its sharp
teeth to rip away the bark, then it hooks
out the grub with its long finger.

AYE-AYE AT RISK
Madagascan people
think that the aye-aye
brings bad luck. Aye-
ayes are now in danger
of becoming extinct
because people have
killed so many of them.

The Madagascan aye-aye
emerges at night to feed
on insect grubs.

Tarsier

Location South-east Asia

Adult size up to 50cm from head to tail

Diet carnivore

Tarsiers are small primates with huge eyes and long fingers and toes. Tarsiers are **nocturnal** animals, which means they are active at night. Their large eyes help them to see in the dark and judge distances as they jump from tree to tree. Tarsiers are good climbers. They use their long fingers and toes to grip on to the bark of trees.

Tarsiers are the world's smallest primates – the same type of animal as monkeys, chimpanzees and people.

Meaty diet

Unlike most other primates, tarsiers do not eat plants. They feast on a wide range of animals – mainly insects but also small birds, reptiles and bats. Tarsiers were once common around the world, but they now live only in the rainforests of South-east Asia.

FREAKY FEATURE

Each eye of the tarsier measures around 1.6cm across – that's bigger than its brain!

Okapi

The okapi's oddest feature is the area of black-and-white stripes on its legs and rump – like a zebra's stripes. But okapis are actually more closely related to giraffes than to zebras. Okapis are shy mammals. They like to hide away in rainforests. Their black-and-white markings help to hide them from their main predator – leopards.

The stripy fur of the okapi may help to camouflage the animal from predators. The stripes blend in with the long grasses of the okapi's forest habitat.

In danger

Okapis are common in zoos around the world, but there are very few of them left in the wild – fewer than 20,000. They are threatened by people who hunt them, and by the destruction of the rainforests where they live.

Location rainforests in Central Africa

Adult size up to 2.5m long

Diet herbivore

Tapir

Tapirs look like pigs, but they are actually more closely related to horses and rhinos. There are four different kinds of tapir, and they all live in tropical rainforests. Tapirs are often found near rivers, and enjoy a dip in the water to cool off. They also use rivers to escape from predators, such as jaguars and tigers. Tapirs are good swimmers, and can dive down to eat plants growing on the riverbed.

Location Central and South America and South-east Asia

Adult size up to 2m long

Diet herbivore

Mobile nose

The most unusual thing about the tapir is its short snout, which can move in all directions. Tapirs use their snouts to pluck berries, fruits and leaves from bushes and trees. Tapirs prefer young, juicy plants because they are easier to digest.

So many tapirs are hunted for their meat and fur that they are now facing extinction.

FREAKY FEATURE

Baby tapirs are born with horizontal stripes, but these disappear as they grow up.

Mandrill

Mandrills are the biggest monkeys in the world. They live in the rainforests of Africa, in large groups. Each group has one **dominant** male, several females and the young mandrills. Most other adult males live alone. Sometimes, different groups join together, forming a troop of hundreds of mandrills. At night, mandrills climb up into the trees to sleep.

Location Africa

Adult size up to 1m long from head to tail

Diet omnivore

Sign of strength

These are really colourful creatures! The bright colours on the nose and rump of the male mandrill show his strength. The dominant males have the brightest colours of all. The females are duller. The colours on their rump may help mandrills to follow each other in the long grass, as they search for food such as fruits, eggs and small mammals.

Mandrills are prey for hungry leopards and pythons.

FREAKY FEATURE

The colours on the male mandrill become brighter as he gets more excited.

Proboscis monkey

Location Borneo, Indonesia

Adult size up to 1.5m, including the tail

Diet herbivore

The proboscis monkey has a really long nose, which is where it gets its name (proboscis is another word for snout). The males have bigger noses than the females. Female proboscis monkeys find males with bigger noses more attractive. Proboscis monkeys spend most of their time up in the trees, but they also like to swim.

The long nose of the male proboscis monkey can reach up to 17.5cm long.

Big bellies

Proboscis monkeys also have big bellies. This is because they have more than one stomach! They eat lots of seeds, fruits and leaves, so they need another stomach to break down the tough plants that they eat.

Pangolin

Pangolins are amazing scaly mammals with no teeth! They use their good sense of smell to find ant hills and termite mounds, then they break them open with their powerful claws and scoop up the termites with their tongue. The pangolin's scales are made of a material called keratin, which is the same substance that makes up our hair and fingernails.

Location Africa and Asia

Adult size biggest species up to 1m long

Diet carnivore

Armour plated

When a pangolin feels threatened, it tucks its face under its tail and rolls up into a tight ball. The overlapping scales are like armour, with razor-sharp edges to keep even the most persistent predators away. As a last line of defence, pangolins can also spray a foul-smelling liquid from a **gland** under their tails.

FREAKY FEATURE

Pangolins have very long tongues, which are covered with sticky saliva to trap ants and termites.

The scaly skin of the pangolin protects the animal from predators such as hyenas and leopards.

Slow loris

The slow loris lives up to its name, because it moves slowly through the trees in the rainforests of South-east Asia. Slow lorises may be slow, but they are good climbers. They have strong hands and feet to creep along the branches. Slow lorises are nocturnal animals, which means they are active at night. During the day, they curl up in a tight ball and sleep in branches high in the treetops.

Busy nights

At night, the slow loris uses its senses of smell, sight and hearing to catch prey such as insects and small vertebrates (animals with backbones). It hides from predators, but if one attacks, the slow loris drops from the branches and rolls into a tight ball.

The slow loris forages at night, feeding on fruits, shoots, eggs and animals.

SLOW BUT DEADLY

The bite of the slow loris is very poisonous. It can even kill a person.

Location South-east Asia

Adult size up to 40cm

Diet omnivore

Fossa

Fossas are the largest meat eaters on the island of Madagascar. They look like cats, but they are more closely related to mongooses and meerkats. Lemurs are the fossa's favourite food. They hunt them by creeping up on them quietly, before chasing them with a quick burst of speed. Fossas also hunt birds and reptiles.

Location Madagascar

Adult size up to 80cm (excluding the tail)

Diet carnivore

The mating game

Fossas have an unusual way of breeding. During the breeding season, females mate with as many males as possible, instead of just one. No one really knows why they do this, but scientists think it allows the healthiest and strongest male to become the father of the young fossas.

The fossa is an endangered species because so much of its rainforest habitat is being destroyed by people.

Raccoon dog

The raccoon dog looks like a raccoon, but it is actually part of the dog family. It is about the same size as a fox, but has shorter legs and a shorter tail. Raccoon dogs will eat almost any type of food, from fruits and seeds to insects, fish, birds, frogs and other small mammals. They will even break open the shells of tortoises to get at the meat inside.

Location East and South-east Asia

Adult size up to 70cm long

Diet omnivore

Warm and dry

In the winter, the raccoon dog has a thick coat of fur and a layer of coarser hairs over it. The fur keeps the raccoon dog warm, which it needs because the temperature can fall below –25°C. The guard hairs make the animal waterproof. The raccoon dog sheds its fur in the summer.

The raccoon dog's thick winter fur will not keep it warm in very cold weather, so it may **hibernate** to stay alive.

FUR TRADE

Its fur makes the raccoon dog very popular with hunters. Raccoon dogs are now farmed for their fur, especially in countries such as China, and their pelts are used to make fur coats.

41

Duck-billed platypus

The duck-billed platypus is a mammal, but an odd one because the females lay eggs. Almost all mammals give birth to babies instead. The platypus's soft-shelled eggs hatch after ten days. The mother then feeds her young with her milk – just like any other mammal. The platypus's snout looks like a duck's bill, but is actually quite soft. It is used for finding food, at night. During the day the platypus sleeps in a burrow.

Super swimmers

The platypus spends most of its time in water. It has a **streamlined** body and webbed feet, which make it an excellent swimmer. It eats insect grubs and other invertebrates (animals without backbones) from the riverbed. Like most mammals, though, it is also covered with warm fur.

The enormous beak of the duck-billed platypus gives this unusual egg-laying mammal its common name.

FREAKY FEATURE

The male platypus is one of the few mammals that can produce poison.

Location eastern Australia and Tasmania

Adult size up to 60cm long

Diet omnivore

Walrus

Location Arctic Ocean

Adult size up to 3.5m long

Diet carnivore

A male walrus breaks the surface of the water to breathe before diving back down to search for food such as crabs.

Walruses are large sea mammals that spend most of their time in shallow seas in the Arctic. They come on land to breed. They are closely related to seals and sea lions, but those animals do not have tusks. Walrus tusks are overgrown teeth. In the largest males they can grow to 1 metre long. Walruses bellow and snort loudly to each other. They have fat on their bodies, to keep them warm in the freezing Arctic.

Breeding colonies

During the breeding season, walruses gather in large groups, called colonies, on the Arctic ice. They use their tusks like pickaxes to haul their huge bodies out of the water and on to the ice. The males fight for the right to mate with the females. They use their long tusks as weapons. The fights are violent and males can get injured, or even killed.

43

Quiz

Now you have read about some of the world's most extraordinary animals, try this fun quiz to see how much you remember. All the answers can be found in the pages of this book. (You can also find them on page 48.)

Scorpion fish

1. How do scorpion fish avoid being eaten by predators? Do they:
a) swim away b) have camouflage
c) have venomous spines
d) all three

2. What is the hammerhead shark's favourite food?
a) rabbits b) seals
c) people d) stingrays

3. Which poisonous fish is a luxury food in some parts of the world?
a) angler fish b) scorpion fish
c) puffer fish d) leafy sea dragon

4. What is the name of the world's largest amphibian?
a) axolotl
b) Chinese giant salamander
c) poison arrow frog d) olm

5. In which type of habitat would you find an olm?
a) ocean b) rainforest
c) cave d) desert

6. The gharial is a relative of which other reptile?
a) crocodile b) snake
c) lizard d) tortoise

7. The thorny devil lives in which type of habitat?
a) rainforest b) ocean
c) desert d) grassland

8. What is the name of the world's smallest bird?
a) peafowl b) bee hummingbird
c) ostrich d) turkey

9. What is the favourite food of the bee hummingbird?
a) leaves b) caterpillars
c) nectar d) snails

10. Which bird has a bony growth on its bill?
a) mallee fowl b) wild turkey
c) bee hummingbird d) hornbill

11. The capybara is the world's largest rodent. Which of these animals is also a rodent?
a) mouse b) hamster
c) naked mole rat d) all three

12. What type of animal is a dugong?
a) fish b) amphibian c) reptile
d) mammal

13. Where would you find a colony of naked mole rats?
a) in the treetops
b) in underground burrows
c) in your home d) in the ocean

14. The aye-aye is a relative of which other type of mammal?
a) monkeys b) gorillas
c) chimpanzees d) all three

15. The okapi is a close relative of which animal?
a) giraffe b) zebra c) tapir d) horse

16. What is the name of the world's largest monkey?
a) spider monkey
b) proboscis monkey
c) mandrill
d) baboon

17. Which animal has a very long tongue to hook ants and termites out of their nests?
a) hornbill b) star-nosed mole
c) dugong d) pangolin

18. The slow loris lives in which type of habitat?
a) rainforest b) desert
c) grassland d) ocean

19. Which of these animals do people farm and hunt for their fur?
a) raccoon dog b) fossa
c) giraffe d) horse

20. Which of these animals is one of the only mammals to lay eggs?
a) capybara b) dugong
c) duck-billed platypus d) walrus

Okapi

Glossary

adaptation when an animal's body changes to help it live longer

amphibians animals with cold blood that live in the water when young but move on to the land as adults

bacteria microscopic animals that can be helpful or harmful

bait food put on a hook to catch a fish or other animal

bird of prey bird that hunts animals for food

breeding season the time in the year when animals mate and produce babies

burrows holes underground dug by animals

camouflage colours and marks on an animal's skin or fur that help it blend in with its surroundings

captivity when an animal is kept by people

carnivore an animal that eats meat

coat of arms symbol that represents a group of people

colonies groups of animals that live together

cold-blooded having blood that changes temperature with the surroundings

crustaceans animals with hard shells that mainly live in water

currents movements in an area of water

dominant describes an animal that rules over other animals

evolve develop and change over a very long period of time

extinct when there are no more of a species left living on Earth

game bird wild bird that is hunted for food

gills slits on a fish's body that it uses to breathe through

gland a body part that produces useful substances

habitats the places where animals live

hatch when young break out of an egg

headdresses elaborate decoration worn on the head

herbivore an animal that eats plants

hibernate to sleep through the winter

infection when bacteria grow inside an animal's body and cause harm

larva the tiny worm-like young form of some animals

mammals animals that feed their young with milk

national bird a bird that is a symbol of a country

nectar the sugary liquid produced by flowers

nocturnal active at night

omnivore an animal that eats both meat and plants

organs large body parts that help an animal live

outback desert in Australia

predators animals that hunt other animals

preening when a bird cleans its feathers using its bill

prey an animal that is hunted by other animals

primates mammals with hands and feet and large brains compared to the size of their bodies

rainforests thick forest habitats where it is warm and wet

reptiles animals with cold blood and scaly bodies

research finding out more about a subject

roost when birds settle to rest

scrubland a habitat that is mostly shrubs

sense the way animals detect things, for example eyesight or hearing

streamlined having a body shape that can cut smoothly through air or water

tadpoles the larvae of amphibians such as frogs

tropical describes the hot regions around the Equator

venom poison produced by some animals such as snakes

warm-blooded having blood that does not change temperature with the surroundings

Further information

Books

Amazing Animals (Dorling Kindersley, 2007)

Amazing Animals from Around the World by Peter Scott (Templar, 2001)

Animals (Record Breakers) by Daniel Gilpin (Wayland, 2010)

Animals at the Edge by Jonathan and Marilyn Baillie (Watts, 2010)

Amazing Animals (Explorers) by Jinny Johnson (Kingfisher, 2010)

My Top 20 Weird Animals by Steve Parker (Miles Kelly Publishing, 2010)

Weird and Wonderful Animals by Brenda Clarke and Helen Orme (Ticktock Media Ltd., 2010)

World's Weirdest Animals by Matt Roper (Summersdale, 2009)

Places to visit

You can see some of these extraordinary animals at a zoo or safari park near you!

Websites

Find out about some of the world's most amazing animals at the BBC CBBC website:

www.bbc.co.uk/cbbc/wild/ amazinganimals

The Guinness Book of World Records website is packed with information about all sorts of record-breaking animals:

www.guinnessworldrecords.com

Meet some more weird and wonderful animals at:

http://oddanimals.com/ unusualanimals.html

Proboscis monkey

Index

Quiz answers   **1.** b&c   **2.** d   **3.** c   **4.** b   **5.** c   **6.** a   **7.** c   **8.** b   **9.** c   **10.** d
11. d   **12.** d   **13.** b   **14.** d   **15.** a   **16.** c   **17.** d   **18.** a   **19.** a   **20.** c